CONSCIOUS ENDURANCE

KHADEJA SHUJA ASHRAFI

AURAQ
PUBLICATIONS

Printed in the Islamic Republic of Pakistan.

Printed: September, 2021
Edition: 1st
ISBN: 978-969-749-138-4
Price: Rs 1000 PKR, $10 US

www.auraqpublications.com | raabta@auraqpublications.com
@AuraqPublications | @AuraqBooks | +92-300-0571-530
Printed and Bound by *Passive Printers* - www.passiveprinters.com

*To My Parents, To Naseem Ahmed Ashrafi And
My Three Best Friends.*

INTRODUCTION

Humans are the most predictable creatures, yet they're unpredictable.

-Infamous

From the very start of our "lessons for life", we're told that we should face the world because there are several phases of life. Time changes, as the good days end and bad days also pass through somehow. Us humans have a very unique tendency to either care about things so much that we lose ourselves or we just don't care at all.

This book is about those phases of life we all go through, but the five parts of this book are divided on the basis of the most common "phase" of our life—how we feel and what happens. We learn something when we fall, but few of us remember the feel. We all are scared to make mistakes and avoid them at all costs, but what about our poor decisions?

What led us to those moments of dark?

How do we rediscover ourselves?

What do we ignore? And Why?

Parts

Part 1

Fight or Flight

Why don't we make right decisions?
Why all bad happens to us?

CONTENTS

Peace

Long tribal enmity was never encouraged
before,

But nowadays, battles are always arranged.

Old, small pueblos and short ways

Everything was allowed other than brawls.

Lively and lovely children were playing.

Everything was fresh; ready with
overwhelming sun,

An air with stress blew, returning indebted
for helping.

Trees were dancing with the joy of serenity,

The leaves were bowing with love,

Pouring the sweetness of luscious fruits.

The branches were dancing with the rhythm
of wind (singing),

The peace was never to be disturbed.

White clouds covering the darkness of the
sky,

Like ever human covering the aggression

With the hunting of love and kindness.

Characters changing their roles like

Chameleons changing colors—some

Red, orange and white.

Sunflowers turning faces towards the sun,

Rose opening, giving the fresh new life of love
and grave.

Just like the long life of trees,

Daffodils blooming towards the sun like the
act of human,

Long road of friendship is to be walked,

Wrapping up the feelings and emotions,
everything ended.

Illusion of Graveyard

In a field, here I stand,

The sky's blue, the grass is trimmed.

It is weird that I see colors and recognize

That motion of the world had not yet stopped.

Now steady I stand, under the blue sky,

Reaper's song sounds like a cry

I know I forget all, but yet,

These faint visions I still get.

The repressed words from those throats,

Fall out like a metaphor

And then I hear cries, weeps and wails,

And suddenly, I feel to be tied by my worst
nightmare.

Then my angel falls, my dreams become true,

My hate for myself and anger grow.

The green grass, I now realize,

Is a demolished graces' view,

But still the motion of the world yet doesn't stop.

Demon Screams

My pain couldn't be subsided
As though nothing had ever happened
The shouts in the dark always echoed
Leaving me all alone
They made me to be pushed and forced.

My destiny all in the darkness
Here's no access towards my ways anymore—
All my dreams in the darkest of grave
No contact with the ones who made it light or
less
Not for even a little time.

As some fairytale, all I have is sour destiny
Now hope to see forward to all gloried canvas
My colors are everywhere spread
Tips of my nails are filled with colorful grime
Now this is what the shout to destine is.

My grief I always left on two
Either on wood or cotton

You think cotton to be always true, but

They are just my thoughts

And the wood—the one my path is crossing though

The things they do or say to me...

Still no solace is seen anywhere near me.

Confined Mortal

Everyone is in a hurry to obtain power,

Only if they know it's going to break them
somehow.

Weaker ones are going to be destroyed,

They die with muffled screams, which are
inaudible sorrows and open wounds.

Power has unseen darkness,

Lays underneath red and bodies—souls
caged, voices broken.

Power is given to the one chosen;

Make your way through the hazy path,
there's long grass you've to cut and pass.

The world beyond is no good,

Blood is splattered on earthly ground.

The novices of the truth have to die,

You have to speak up or at least try.

War Ground

A loft, where is wrapped-around dead or decay.

A wondrous spell chants around its laminated crevices.

Several ways in, but there's no out.

A maze of destiny it is, every time it changes.

A blackened dark heart in a bloodied, wounded chest.

It's a black-and-white vision of a prison.

There's heavy mist on my mind.

I'm either walking dead or am decayed.

But still, I'm here.

My feet is swollen by snake bites.

Witch's burning spells, taking down the lofty fortress.

The darkness around the island is like of every person's inside.

The clock here never strikes twelve.

It's a never-ending dream of hell.

It will steam away in a few seconds.

Graveyard

At the graveyard, I ran for long,

To get away from those light figures;

They follow me like the past horrors.

My mind shuts with a panic attack,

And like that those ghosts trap me in a sack;

They now pull me towards the way back.

I wept like I never had,

My eyes became red;

During this all, I try to think I'm still in my
bed.

It's so bad that life plays such games,

We are born free but are chained

With feelings, relations and later by
competitions.

Part 2

Rehabilitation

Can we live with past?

CONTENTS

What Am I Now?

It's not as I have wanted to be,
A life working both physically and mentally.

I wanted them all at least contented with me,
Every day with a hope n' aim.

No one having sympathy or pity on me,
And let me live or die as I want, eventually.

I have not changed, though many don't agree;
Anguish is what I now feel mostly.

I don't know if anything is left of me;
After all, my heart, like else is burnt already.

My heart broken, my soul shaken,
But I gather every piece very gently.

Now I'm so happy,
That it feels almost freaky.

How sorrows travel

Pain is seeping out of my ripped heart

Thoughts are running through my green
dark.

The sky darkens suddenly

The sky above darkens and cracks slowly

My heart is like massive old machine

Regrets and sorrows change into anger and
rage.

My mind understands and let the heart rule

It knows that heart, out of chest, never rules.

Words with feelings aren't fancy for speakers

Writings of young ones are not liked by adult
readers.

Sorrows are just known by elders, like in life

Young ones become strong without thunders

The muted ones never open their beaks

But from inside, they're not weak.

Sorrows repressed inside are like bad dreams

The glass shatters and we wake with deathly screams.

How sorrows survive afterlife

Climbing my way upwards
Towards hardy success,
My way towards the sky
Seems too hazy and worthless.

Before life can even enter heart,
It's killed by the regrets of past
The sky seems too dark without any spark
It almost feels there's no path.

Does anyone even hear me,
Through all that storms and shouts?
There I'm now, where no one knows,
Is even a door out to my freedom?

I'm struck there and there,
Where neither light sets nor a thunder's
heard
It's like to be in a dark room
A cage so small with no space to move.

I can't move, not even complain

My mouth's shut with tape

My mind is blocked with the wall

Full of images of ages

Don't know why they don't forget.

It's a long, long ago

But I explain my mistakes in a row

Still no one takes it and have mercy

They just push and oppress until you're
stressed.

Smash you like trash and throw you in the
bin

And press the nerves that you don't know
have ever been

'My dear, be your best or do smile'

So that they lose and you have happiness in
embrace.

Scarf of Misery

Destiny is incomplete
Without despair and misery as a riddle
Where happiness is a feeble needle.

Happiness is lost in a plush carpet
We think it as an expended velvet.

But remember, when happiness is found,
You're already bleeding
But great is you don't feel the wound.

Happiness is truly a bush of rose
You have to walk through needles to pursue.

Ashes, Mirror, Fake

In this life at the porch of heart,

The blood from there circulating so fast.

As I see my eyes in those transformed
mirrors,

They seem clear but very broken.

Those had seen so much that they even,

Didn't even break from unseen pressure.

I try to not inflict that upon it,

As it's the only thing I see—I be...

No, not that I am and from inside,

Yes, that's the deepest, more than ocean.

My best option to drown inside that blue,

That's difficult but there's some true.

The world would stop so soon,

It would take just a little sparks.

And we will all die, while we're alive,

The fire surely of hate, jealously and
vengeance.

The green that grows on sapphire grounds,
They will darken to block ash, not so soon.
They will, if not burn then, bury inside,
Like someone opened ground and then closed
it.

The heavenly roses, once they bloomed,
Have darkened from blood and gloom.

Pure Sin

Black butterflies cover up the sky.

Walking on that road is a maximum trial.

Words fly up, they're the symbol for the sin of communication.

To disclose the portal of knowledge, you have to fly up the tree of pine.

Reading those very lines take a lot of time,

But to ignore those wonderful passages is a tiny crime.

Time gives wounds, so incurable.

It travels like Amazon on fire.

That path is so dark, not even a moth can pass.

Now you know it's better to sit on dark grass.

Part 3

Life

After all, what is life?
Why we love it?

CONTENTS

Words on me

Where are my smiles, where is that life?
Here I'm standing in broad light.
Blinding my eyes from the straight sunlight.
Here I'm standing towards the right.

On my back, I hear the chit chat—the gossip.
Some on me, some on others like me.
I try to block my ears but then see all flip.
Then everything's black and I can't see.

Light just drips from the ceiling through
crevices.
And I see then back and forth,
I see where I live,
It's the cage where everything finishes.

It's the cage where I live,
Where you deny to hear or see anything.

Inside my heart

At the pit of that bloody sponge,

There, where all the feelings generate,

Where from I want to run, from white as it
feels so bright,

To run from the right and say so to love alike,

I have it captured inside; inside it will rot,

I fought my urges and cries and also frights.

Ever got nothing: deceive, agony, anger and
aggression,

I closed eyes to all that;

I fought the nearness of time towards

The things, events, dates or even those days.

I don't ever wanna feel it or see it again,

But all my insights shows me those dark
sights again and again.

Oh Allah, O God, where do I go?

How can I grow as a right pupil?

My love, my passion, my obsession kept
inside that little box,

No one let me out or let me shout my fears.

Grounds of affection where could I found?

All I do is never for me but for the ones
around,

I want to be alone, but am not allowed.

The way out of all this can't be found,

Light and light is all over.

It's too much for me to open my eyes,

It's too difficult to stop my cries.

I now see no way for myself,

I want to break out the barriers, shed those
tears.

There, in all those barren grounds,

There, I can let all my sorrow out.

Where I will be empty surrounded by night,

I would do my last heart fight;

And surely try to get away

From all the bad, dark and towards my life's
spark.

Sunrise

As the visuals of serenity fades,

The message of the moment sets.

Like the sun rising, the intellect of a person
heightens.

Someone's memory saddens, someone's
distance heightens.

A few times it is blunt to say a lot and a few
to say the truth.

Life has its own hills, the mortgage of high is
the peace of low.

Voices tatters in winds at the meadow, I sat.

The waters of the rivers are same as my good
times.

But my faith in life never shatters.

As the visuals of serenity fades,

The message of the moment sets.

Like the sun rising, the intellect of a person
heightens.

Inside Me

It's all and all my huge secret,

I've always tried to revive my inner sight.

Those scenes of war inside me,

Still inside me like an unsheathed sword.

Scenes hidden inside the leather walls

Are not to be disclosed.

It's all my or if like me, others' role.

If these secrets are ever to emerge,

It scatters dark, disdain, disappointment,
disapproval and then it decomposes.

If those feelings are too open, "it should be
precise."

If too brief, "I can't understand, why or how
or if…"

44

It's shown as either they don't know,

Or they can't believe.

But I know all embankments of disbelief.

Dead Moon

The monsters under my bed scare me no more.

Like they also had lost my worth.

The fear of being under gratitude has now subsided.

Leaving me with the debts of doings so unknown to me.

Life and time now seem to have a lot in common.

My faltered emotions are now running in my teared veins.

Sour words of bewildered wild,

Cut through me, giving the sheer pleasure to mortal beings.

Mental awareness of those nasty quirks isn't enough.

Now the world has to open the locked doors of justification.

Past

With all the sync by which I talk and laugh,
No one wonders about my past.

It is a miracle in this world that,
People although being hurt, hurt others.

I love the fall of dark of closed eyes;
While open, my eyes hurt from shattered
windows of peace.

Start of Destruction

Every word around me is not a word.

Every word I write I want it to be word.

Now I try to speak, but there is no voice.

I'm not too loud these times.

The time may be dark, but, I see no light even
from a foe.

The demons of my heart recreate.

My memories of the past suffocate.

Is this the time? Or my mind?

All I see are endless days.

Word is—words so true—the storm of
sadness, I now brew.

Part 4

Realization or Dawn

Is it too late?
What have I done?
What did I learn?

CONTENTS

Puzzle

Arranging the puzzle of quirky puddle,

It's a puzzle that couldn't be ever rematched;

So it be only a wonder

These are always illusion to those, so
unknown

But among them, one do know how to
arrange.

This *one* had already imagined.

The *one* he is, too lonely and too lazy,

People always don't like its content, say "it's
too dreamy."

Liars

Everyone says they know the truth of life,

But they solemnly, cruelly lie.

Everyone knows it more than other,

But this is also a lie.

They all know the same,

But lie to not be ashamed.

They lie to make their words intense,

Forgetting how much the situation was
already tense.

The difference is, some are more dark in
shade,

But the truth is;

The impact of deceive never fades.

 The one lighter in shade,

Aren't really for now illiterate.

Maybe they seem to be cool and fit,

But there are always two fish in the lake.

Either their pitch is low or they're not a pro,

Sage's Passages

Ages ago, there was what we call sages,
There wit and stories, people wrote for wages.

In their times, their stories were far away
news
Now we reminisce it and be amuse.

The witty one is the one condemning their
rages,
Elegant is the one without dual faces.

Walk behind the one going to the right way,
Obscure the wealth of knowledge every day.

Always remember to work hard and pray,
And never forget that success in not given in
a tray.

Shaded Leaves

Time flies like dead leaf on a windy day,
Life turns away furiously from us prey.

The decent spirit of a human is like water,
It changes in the shape of whatever infortune
life scatters.

May our black holes never be healed,
Because it makes us run on life's reel.

You'll fly higher and higher in your bubble;
Don't forget it's a thought of your brain.
O you sturdy human! Embrace the
uncertainties of quite certain.

Devil only implies his hateful gratitude on
those,
Who sing merry of his goodness by prose.

Confused Freedom

Birds fly high up the sky, they sing praises of freedom,

But mighty human is trapped; this is the vile value of power.

In greed, to fly high, we forget ourselves;

To fly high, we perforate our hearts with poisonous knives.

Mind of a human undergoes so many disturbances,

That when people know it, they fake hurtful or pitied faces.

You're egoistic and arrogant, this is what they whine,

I confirm them affirmatively to make their assumptive mind a little satisfied.

They don't think of my heart, I can't see their good,

They don't hear my words and I don't take them as independent birds.

Education on spirits

Green lives cling to brown souls,

Green that is life, grants access to human life.

Lives and *soul,* don't you know what they are?

Neither are they beauty of moon nor are they voices of birds.

They are what produce the fuel for your stomach and oxygen to breath,

They are your dark life; somehow the lesson of your existence.

They are what birds live on,

Still you deny their beauty.

You selfish beings praise the beauty of the heartless,

Yet, you laugh at what beats your heart.

Even its shadow gives you comfort,
Those are the friends of friendless.

59

Khadeja Shuja Ashrafi

Mother Nature

Is my intro still so low?

Don't you remember your forgotten foe?

Oh Allah! Give us the love of your nature,

Thou make me seem blind; Tell me am I?

They laugh at me for loving those lovers of life,

O God! Am I blind or they don't have eyes?

Those trees, their flowers, their fruit and that grass,

They are my most memorable timepass.

Just a Foe

If people have to come and go,

Why they become our temporary foe?

Relations are like day and night—one comes
other goes,

A human's life cycle is like a Ferris wheel,
You go up and down until the life is out.

There are meetings and departures, but soon
friends get farther;

Although we trust all that, we see but not all
is true.

Once there is love, unity and harmony, but
not long gone, a long feud.

Realization

Those late realizations of life,

Those juvenile decisions of time,

The wounds of the soul are like anopheles'
bites.

The depths of oceans,

The shudders of breeze,

The liveliness from love is a true bliss.

Times of the day, hours of night,

Those all mistakes learnt by time,

Tell you the worth of life.

Anyhow, you can fly like an eagle,

Sometimes roar like a lion,

But doesn't that matter; you're still in a
prison.

Even if you swim along and survive the
storm,

The trauma it imbibes will never fade away.

Part 5

The End

I've just start to understand.
It's too early.
I've gotten all my answers.

CONTENTS

Sweet Decay

The moths are shining in the night sky.

The world is seeming all too bright.

It's uncertain, it's creepy; everyone is so sweet.

As sweet as honey, directly from beehive.

I have a feeling as queer as certainty.

That I'm too exposed, too futile as a pointless fight.

I yearn to not be too veer or be a bit diligent.

The night I described afore was not so dark.

People who are like day, always try to conceal the shine of the stars.

Everyone thinks if you say a bit, you don't have secrets.

But what they don't know is you're a flaunt bird.

Too Young

They think that I'm too young to understand anything.

Only if they know how much pain I'm in.

My heart beats in my chest, don't they know?

I'm alive in front of them like concrete.

Are there the ways my sins can sing or is it just because of me?

Now nothing really excites me; there's always a dark sheet.

I feel like slipping in my hand, as it never has slipped away.

They drink my joy like a vampire, like I'm not a human—just a prey.

My eyes have gotten numb, my heart beats a lot.

The drink they enjoy, is it my blood?

Life Is a Tree

Tours of the dark, I have done a lot,

Things are too painful, I've suffered a lot.

I fall down, every now and then,

Like the leaves in autumn

Though they're free and can fly.

Standing on the dead cliff, I fall down.

At last, someday I'll vanish,

It would be more like being banished.

Now I can't control my life or thoughts,

Both are bending like the trees are too tall.

My love is for life and beautiful sunshine,

Will never be vanished by the passage of
time.

My roots are deep underground,

My brain would've stopped, from the lack of
light.

It pains me to seek and see,

Other trees are lower than me, to be

Successful, fulfilled, calmed, in ecstasy.

Because it's odd, that success is my fantasy.

Darkness can also be bright

Singing of birds, chanting of leaves,

Night fades as the sun breaks.

The singing of birds or it's cold breeze,

The clashes of water, the swimming fishes,

Humans are around with hearts so broken.

If herbs can be life, then darkness can also
be bright.

Why do those trees seem to cry like they
know all?

Their tears, the rotten leaves break with the
gentle breeze,

They glide through the wind and approach to
their graves,

As they've lived enough in shadowy caves.

Leaves, like humans, do also fade.

Nature of Life

Deadly shallows with clumsy fellows,

There is nothing, otherwise a dark sheet.

But somehow a twinkle of light,

Absorbed colors but nothing to change,

Wherever they are, I am out of place.

Never understand the shape of leaf,

I am on the branch, not yet free.

Darkness is green nor black; the world is
seeming out of track,

Nothing far, but closer.

Every night is becoming colder,

Sun doesn't shine so bright as in the eyes of
innocence.

Clouds are passing by with wind being shy,

This path is what mind had directed.

Water is running out of place,

Eyes are red with the rise of dark.

Life is out, but nothing is in,

But the cycle of life never runs in my right.

All the way down the hill,

There is no sway of eating all my old sins.

Printed and Bound by *Passive Printers* - www.passiveprinters.com
Printing press that offers Print on Demand (POD) Facility.
Printed in The Islamic Republic of Pakistan.